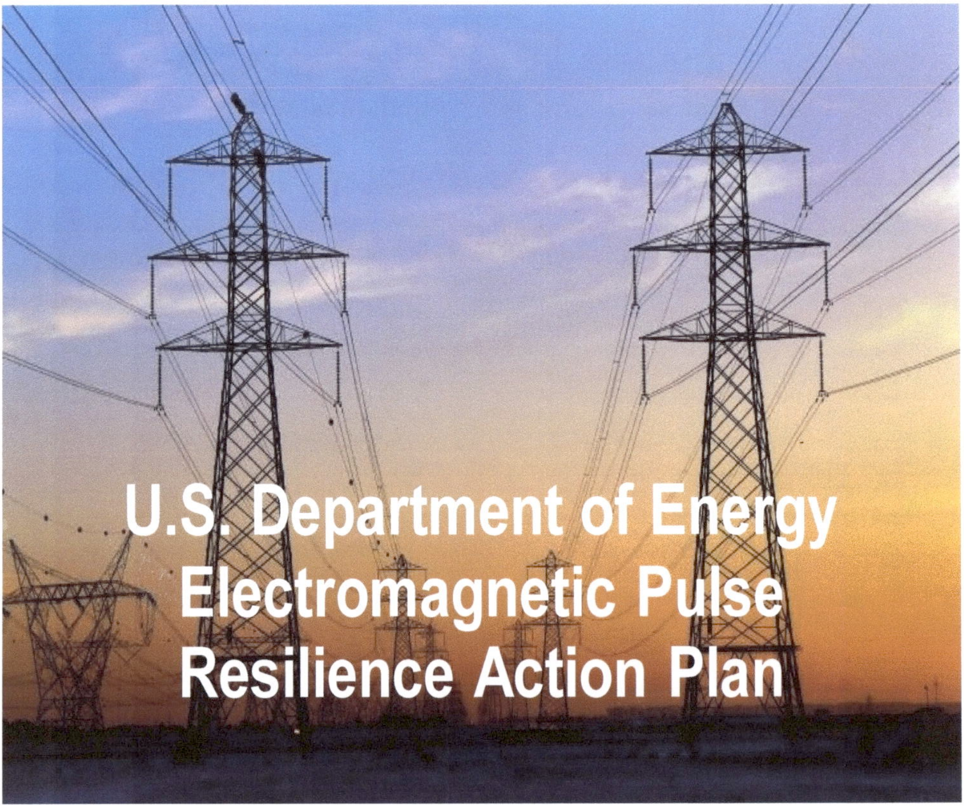

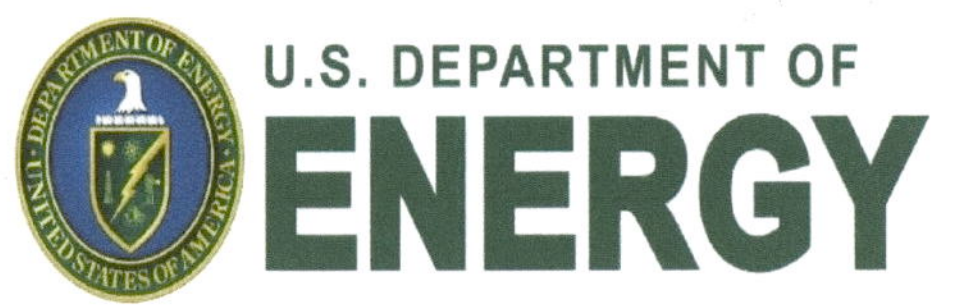


JANUARY 2017

I0791055

# DOE Electromagnetic Pulse Resilience Action Plan

## For Further Information

This document was prepared by the Infrastructure Security and Energy Restoration Division (ISER) of the U.S. Department of Energy's Office of Electricity Delivery and Energy Reliability (OE) under the direction of Patricia Hoffman, Assistant Secretary, and Devon Streit, Deputy Assistant Secretary.

Specific questions about this document may be directed to John Ostrich (john.ostrich@hq.doe.gov) or Puesh Kumar (puesh.kumar@hq.doe.gov) who lead the Risk and Hazards Analysis Program in ISER.

Contributors include the Idaho National Laboratory and other Department of Energy (DOE) National Laboratories, as well as government and industry partners.

Special thanks to Dr. George Baker, Ms. Lisa Bendixen, and Dr. William Tedeschi.

# DOE Electromagnetic Pulse Resilience Action Plan

## Table of Contents

# DOE Electromagnetic Pulse Resilience Action Plan

# DOE Electromagnetic Pulse Resilience Action Plan

## Introduction

### Background on EMP

Electromagnetic pulses (EMPs) are intense pulses of electromagnetic energy resulting from solar-caused effects or man-made nuclear and pulse-power devices. Of these, nuclear EMP has the most ubiquitous effects because of the combination of its broadband nature and large area coverage. Nuclear EMP has the demonstrated potential to disrupt, damage, or destroy a wide variety of electrical and electronic equipment. The strength and area coverage of nuclear EMP environments depends on the warhead type and yield, and the altitude and latitude of the detonation. A nuclear device detonated at altitudes between 30 and 400 kilometers generates an EMP with amplitudes in the tens of kilovolts per meter with a radius of effects from hundreds to thousands of kilometers. This high-altitude EMP (also known as HEMP) effect couples to and can disable electrical and electronic systems in general, but poses the highest risks to long-line networks, including electric power and long-haul communications. Although an EMP is also generated by low altitude or surface bursts (referred to as source region EMP or SREMP), the affected area is localized compared to a HEMP. For this reason, this action plan focuses on larger-scale EMP events produced by high altitude detonations.

A HEMP event includes three waveforms: E1, E2, and E3. The E1 waveform is a fast (nanosecond rise time, hundreds of nanoseconds duration), broad-band pulse that disrupts systems in general, including long-line electrical systems, computers, sensors, and electronic-based control systems. The E2 waveform is longer and much lower in amplitude than the E1 waveform and manifests itself by enhancing the EMP currents on long lines in the microsecond and millisecond regime. E2 current pulses are comparable to currents induced by nearby lightning strikes. The E3 waveform is a low-amplitude, long-duration pulse, persisting for hundreds of seconds that induces currents in long power and communication lines, destabilizing or damaging connected equipment such as transformers and solid state communication line drivers. E3 waveform effects are comparable to those from solar geomagnetic effects. Most conversations about EMP focus on either E1, the large initial energy pulse, or E3, the smaller and longer duration effect, but to properly address EMP, all portions of the waveform must be considered.

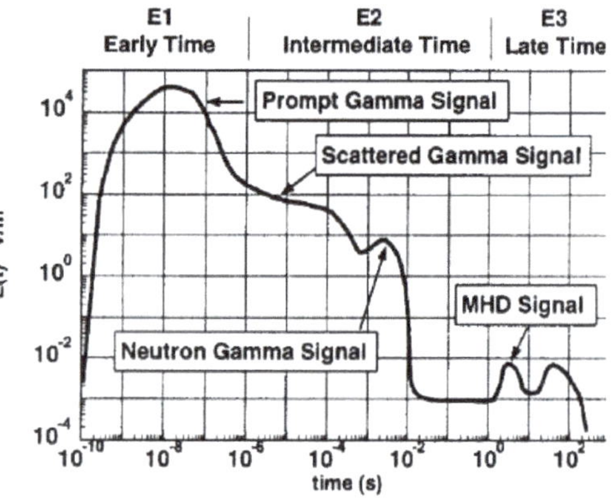


Figure 1. EMP Environment: DOD MIL-STD-464A

# DOE Electromagnetic Pulse Resilience Action Plan

## The Joint EMP Resilience Strategy

In response to increased concern about the potential impacts to the electric grid from a HEMP, in late 2015, the Secretary of Energy directed the development of an EMP resilience strategy in coordination with the electric power industry. In January 2016, the U.S. Department of Energy (DOE) began work with the Electric Power Research Institute (EPRI) to develop such a strategy. The *Joint Electromagnetic Pulse Resilience Strategy*[1] (Joint Strategy) was released in July 2016. The development of the Joint Strategy was a public-private collaborative effort, designed to establish a common framework with consistent goals and objectives that will guide both government and industry efforts to increase grid resilience to EMP threats.

Central to the development of the Joint Strategy was an effort to enhance shared government-industry understanding of the current status of risks from, and preparedness for, HEMP events. This is of particular importance, as will be discussed later in this document, because much of what is currently known about EMP effects to the grid is extrapolated from computer models designed for other purposes (e.g., understanding Department of Defense (DoD) system effects), or is classified and thus difficult to share with industry.

The Joint Strategy identified five strategic goals:

1. Improve and Share Understanding of EMP: Threat, Effects, and Impacts
2. Identify Priority Infrastructure
3. Test and Promote Mitigation and Protection Approaches
4. Enhance Response and Recovery Capabilities to an EMP Attack
5. Share Best Practices Across Government and Industry, Nationally and Internationally

### Current DOE Efforts to Improve EMP Resilience

In 2016, DOE had five EMP resilience-related projects underway, including the development of the Joint Strategy and DOE Action Plan.

- **Methodology to Assess HEMP Impact on the Electric Grid (Oak Ridge National Laboratory).** This project is developing an approach to assess the damage created by an EMP device that transmission planners can use for planning. The results will include a probabilistic model of bulk power system response under an EMP event, using previous research and established power systems evaluation techniques and will characterize typical SCADA and protection hardware in time domain and frequency domain.

- **EMP/GMD Impacts Study (Los Alamos National Laboratory).** This study is leveraging the best currently available experimental data; device, equipment, and system models; and simulation tools to determine EMP and GMD events of concern. This study is focusing primarily on the bulk electric power system including large generating stations, large power transformers, the transmission network, and transmission system protection. Electrical distribution systems may potentially be included, if warranted, after consideration of the consequences for the bulk power system.

- **Report on Vulnerability of and Impact to Grid from an EMP (Idaho National Laboratory).** This project on the vulnerability of the grid to an EMP will identify the potential impact on reliability and delivery of electric power. The report will address protective and mitigation measures for these vulnerabilities, including hardening of infrastructure, blocking of induced currents and voltages, stocking and prepositioning of spare parts, and operational and emergency planning.

- *Joint Electromagnetic Pulse Resilience Strategy* **(DOE, EPRI, ICF).** The Joint Strategy was designed to establish a common framework with consistent goals and objectives to guide both government and industry efforts to increase grid resilience to EMP threats. (See text.)

- **U.S. Department of Energy** *Electromagnetic Pulse Resilience Action Plan* **(Idaho National Laboratory and other DOE National Labs, ICF).** The DOE Action Plan is intended to guide DOE's EMP resilience research and development (R&D) activities for the next five years. *(See text.)*

---

[1] http://www.energy.gov/sites/prod/files/2016/07/f33/DOE_EMPStrategy_July2016_0.pdf

# DOE Electromagnetic Pulse Resilience Action Plan

## EMP Action Plans

Following development of the Joint Strategy, both DOE and EPRI committed to developing separate, but coordinated, Action Plans that would implement the five strategic goals. EPRI's plan focused on those actions that industry would undertake to mitigate EMP risks; DOE's plan (this Action Plan) delineates the steps that DOE will take to address EMP risks. Although the two Action Plans were developed independently, DOE and EPRI collaborated closely to ensure that the plans complement one another and avoid duplication of effort.

The U.S. infrastructure for electric power generation, transmission, and distribution is predominately owned by private industry and thus its protection lies largely in their hands. In recognition of this, EPRI's industry-focused EMP Action Plan was developed in support of its member companies and the Electricity Subsector Coordinating Council (ESCC),[2] and it was designed to inform industry investment decisions. The research that is outlined in the EPRI EMP Action Plan is scheduled for completion over the next three years.

DOE's Action Plan, by contrast, emphasizes the Federal government's ability to clarify and communicate EMP threats and impacts, reduce HEMP vulnerabilities and facilitate the energy sector's response and recovery after HEMP events. While the focus of this plan is on protection from and mitigation of HEMP effects, many of the actions proposed herein can be scaled to address high-power radio-frequency weapon (RFW) events that may impact a smaller area than a HEMP event and are also relevant to geomagnetic disturbances (GMD)[3] which are similar in system interaction and effects to the E3 portion of the nuclear EMP waveform. Table 1 below compares many of the attributes of EMP and GMD for greater context.

The DOE Action Plan was developed with input from interagency partners, the DOE National Laboratories, and the electric utility industry, in part through a one-day session with more than 50 EMP and electric power industry experts, to identify, discuss, and prioritize potential action items within the context of the five goals of the Joint EMP Resilience Strategy. Experts were also brought in individually to identify and discuss potential action items. An initial set of suggested action items was then developed by the Idaho National Laboratory with support from the Los Alamos, Sandia, Oak Ridge, and Lawrence Livermore National Laboratories.

A subsequent working group enhanced the document and compared the action items with the recommendations made in several major studies that address the EMP threat, such as the 2008 EMP Commission[4] and the 2015 Jewish Institute for National Security Affairs (JINSA) Gemunder Center EMP Task Force[5] reports. Recommendations from these and other studies were

---

[2] The ESCC serves as the principal liaison between the Federal government and the electric power sector, with the mission of coordinating efforts to prepare for, and respond to, national-level disasters or threats to critical infrastructure.

[3] In 2015, DOE worked closely with officials in the White House Office of Science and Technology Policy, other Federal agencies, and international partners, to discuss and develop a Space Weather Strategy and an Action Plan to improve preparedness of the nation to GMD events. DOE has many actions planned over the next several years in support of this strategy.

[4] There were 15 recommendations related directly to the electric power system in the 2008 EMP Commission report. DOE's Action Plan at least partially addresses 11 of these. DOE's Action Plan does not specifically mention quick fixes, does not address telecommunications directly, does not *assure* protection of electricity assets, and does not mention the need to assure an adequate number of recovery personnel. Report of the Commission to Assess the Threat to the United States from Electromagnetic Pulse (EMP) Attack, Critical National Infrastructures, April 2008. http://www.empcommission.org/docs/A2473-EMP_Commission-7MB.pdf

[5] DOE's Action Plan has action items to address at least part of 12 of the 15 recommendations of the JINSA report as it relates to the bulk electric system and one of the participants in the JINSA task force was part of the previously mentioned working group. The DOE Action Plan does not address the two recommendations related to deterrence, nor does it touch on the one related to

# DOE Electromagnetic Pulse Resilience Action Plan

considered when determining DOE's final recommended action items. The working group obtained reviews from the participants in the earlier one-day session. DOE then revised the contents accordingly, addressed comments, and prioritized and vetted the final set of action items with EMP experts in order to finalize the DOE Action Plan.

**Table 1. EMP versus GMD Characteristics**

| Attribute | EMP | GMD |
|---|---|---|
| Cause | Adversarial threat | Natural hazard |
| Warning | Strategic: unknown<br>Tactical: none to several minutes | Strategic: 18 to 72 hours<br>Tactical: 20 to 45 minutes |
| Effects | *E1:* High peak field – quick rise time<br>*E2:* Medium peak field<br>*E3:* low peak field, but quicker rise time and higher field than for GMD (possibly 3 times higher) | No comparable E1 wave forms<br>No comparable E2 wave forms<br>*E3:* low peak field – fluctuating magnitude and direction |
| Duration | *E1:* less than a 1 microsecond<br>*E2:* less than 10 millisecond<br>*E3 Blast:* ~10 seconds<br>*E3 Heave:* ~1 – 2 minutes | No comparable E1 wave forms<br>No comparable E2 wave forms<br>*E3:* hours |
| Equipment at Risk | *E1:* telecommunications, electronics and control systems, relays, lightning arrestors<br>*E2:* lightning: power lines and tower structures – "flashover", telecommunications, electronics, controls systems, transformers.<br>*E3:* transformers and protective relays – long run transmission and communication - generator step-up transformers | *E3:* transformers and protective relays – long-haul transmission and communications – generator step-up transformers |
| Footprint | Regional to continental depending on height of burst | Regional to worldwide, depending upon magnitude |
| Geographic Variability | Can maximize coverage for E1 or E3<br>*E3:* intensity increases at the lower latitudes and as distance from ground zero is decreased or as yield is increased | *E3:* intensity increases near large bodies of water and generally at higher latitudes although events have been seen in southern latitudes |

## Structure of the DOE Action Plan

This Action Plan is structured to address each of the five strategic goals defined in the Joint Strategy. For each goal, the Action Plan describes a series of actions that will be taken to further the resilience of the grid to HEMP effects. In total, 19 actions are planned. For each action, this Plan identifies specific deliverables and suggested due dates, as well as key partners. Actions related to each strategic goal are grouped together as many of the actions build upon one another and will be performed in parallel to achieve benefits more quickly.

Progress in achieving the full set of goals and objectives of the Joint Strategy and the actions identified in this and the EPRI Action Plan also depends on the commitment of both government

insurance. Deterrence is viewed as a Government-wide responsibility, not exclusively a DOE role. Insurance was not covered since much of the industry is self-insured. *Addressing Electromagnetic Threats to U.S. Critical Infrastructure. JINSA's Gemunder Center EMP Task Force.* September 2015. http://www.jinsa.org/files/EMPreport.pdf

and industry resources. DOE and EPRI will continue to hold meetings with other partners in government and industry to coordinate efforts with these stakeholders as well.

> **Note:** The actions specified in the DOE EMP Resilience Action Plan are intended to inform the policy development process and are not intended as a budget document. The commitment of DOE resources to support these activities will be determined in conjunction with other resource allocation priorities.

## 1. Improve and Share Understanding of EMP: Threat, Effects, and Impacts

Given the concerns over evolving EMP threats, an accurate, science-based understanding of what an EMP event could do to electric power systems is important. And because EMPs have the potential to simultaneously affect multiple parts of the system over large areas, knowledge of the possible impacts of EMP events on discrete components of electricity control, generation, transmission, and distribution, as well as on larger networks of these components, is necessary.

The Federal government (specifically DOD and DOE) has investigated EMP effects broadly for decades and the DOE's National Laboratories[6] have some of the world's most knowledgeable experts on this threat. However, much of the knowledge and understanding of the threat is based upon testing a prior generation of devices and components, some of which are being replaced with newer technologies that have not been adequately tested for EMP impacts. In addition, the three waveforms comprising the EMP environment have been studied separately (with the most attention on the E1 and E3 waveforms), leaving questions about their combined effects. Modeling has provided some information and insights; however, available models are limited in scope and have not been validated via testing.

The following objectives support the joint goal of improving and sharing understanding of EMP threat, effects, and impacts:

- Develop a more complete and current understanding of the threat.
- Disseminate results to industry.
- Expand industry collaboration.
- Improve assessment, modeling, and prediction of equipment and system vulnerabilities and damage.
- Improve assessment, modeling, and prediction of EMP impacts.

To address this joint goal, DOE is planning the following actions: 1) generate a shared understanding of potential EMP effects; 2) identify gaps in EMP knowledge; 3) coordinate government-industry information sharing; 4) develop unclassified composite E1/E2/E3 waveforms for use by industry in modeling/testing their systems; 5) provide an understanding of the susceptibility of specific critical electric grid components to EMP waveforms; 6) evaluate interactive EMP system and component modeling capabilities; 7) develop realistic risk-based EMP planning scenarios for use by industry for planning purposes and assess/model expected damage for each scenario; and 8) report on potential issues of concern for critical infrastructure from the loss of off-site utility power from EMP.

---

[6] The first laboratories began as efforts to support the Manhattan Project during World War II. DOE is now steward to 17 National Laboratories, some of which have served as the leading institutions for scientific innovation in the United States for more than seventy years. More information on the National Laboratories can be found at http://www.energy.gov/about-national-labs.

# DOE Electromagnetic Pulse Resilience Action Plan



## 1.1 Generate a shared understanding of potential EMP effects

Currently, there is little common understanding among Federal, State, industry, National Laboratory, academic, and other stakeholders regarding HEMP threats, potential system effects, and likely consequences. A common understanding is a necessary foundation for both industry and government to address EMP threats and build mitigation strategies in the most strategic way. To this end, DOE will work in collaboration with DOD, the DOE National Laboratories, the Office of the Director of National Intelligence (ODNI) and other members of the intelligence community, including DOE's Office of Intelligence and Counterintelligence, to develop a commonly held understanding of current EMP effects. This common "informational baseline" will help align the efforts of key partners in Government, the National Laboratories, the electric power industry, and other interdependent sectors. This alignment will facilitate coordinated remediation programs and investment decisions.

A significant challenge to developing such a common view is the inability to communicate classified threat information for use in an unclassified public setting. As a result, several EMP tabletop exercises involving utility industry representatives have been conducted without the benefit of intelligence community threat information. A critical component of this action will therefore be the development of materials that allow for a meaningful understanding of the threat and potential impacts, but are not limited by the inclusion of classified information. A forum enabling a stakeholder dialogue with the intelligence community will also be essential for the development of these common materials.

*Deliverable 1.1.1:* Maintain classified and unclassified briefing materials that address the current understanding of the potential impacts of high and low impact EMPs on the electric grid.
*Due Date:* 12/31/2016

*Deliverable 1.1.2:* Create a schedule of industry, interagency, and cross-sector briefings using these materials.
*Due Date:* 03/31/2017

## 1.2 Identify gaps in EMP knowledge

As stated earlier, gaps exist within the current understanding of EMP and its effects on the electric power grid. For example, DOE and industry lack experience on exactly how EMPs affect the high-voltage, heavy-duty equipment in substations and generation plants that are essential to grid operation. DOD has the most experience and best database on EMP effects, but their system focus has been on command, control, communication, and computer systems (C4) which are analogous to the electric power grid monitoring and control systems, but not to high voltage systems organic to generation facilities and substations. Additionally, a number of DOE National Laboratories possess relevant information and data sets and capabilities. To consolidate this information, DOE will work with EPRI and the electric power

# DOE Electromagnetic Pulse Resilience Action Plan

industry, the DoD, the Federal Mission Executive Council (MEC)[7] and individual DOE National Laboratories to identify gaps in the understanding of the environments, system coupling, and impacts of HEMP threats to the electric power system, including generation and transmission assets and system load.

> *Deliverable 1.2.1:* Establish a working group of the Mission Execution Council to identify current gaps in EMP knowledge among the National Laboratories and other Federal agencies.
> *Due Date:* 10/31/2016

> *Deliverable 1.2.2:* Produce a report documenting MEC findings.
> *Due Date:* 12/31/2016

### 1.3 Coordinate government-industry information sharing

Coordination and information sharing between government and industry will be essential to an EMP-resilient grid. Concurrent with the efforts describe in this DOE Action Plan, the electric utility industry, guided by the EPRI-developed Action Plan, will continue its efforts to understand and mitigate EMP threats. Additionally, other sectors such as the financial services sector and the telecommunications sectors, have begun to consider what actions they should take to address EMP threats. Initial work on EMP indicates that the telecommunications sector is also at significant risk from the EMP threat. For this reason, coordinating this broader community to include those knowledgeable of and affected by EMP is important to a national effort to protect critical and interdependent infrastructures. DOE will serve as the lead agency for coordinating interagency and industry information on EMP effects and impacts.

> *Deliverable 1.3.1:* Establish an EMP information working group in coordination with EPRI, the ESCC, and appropriate stakeholders.
> *Due Date:* 12/31/2016

### 1.4 Develop unclassified composite E1/E2/E3 waveforms for use by industry in modeling/ testing their systems

Industry's efforts to understand how EMP will affect specific portions of the grid could be improved through the use of modeling that replicates the specific details of the E1/E2/E3 waveform (including both time signature and power spectrum). However, the only officially-issued U.S. EMP threat environment waveform is classified. To assist industry, DOE will work with the Defense Threat Reduction Agency (DTRA), DoD Laboratories, and the DOE National Laboratories to synthesize existing classified and unclassified test results. Results include those from tests directed by The Commission to Assess the Threat to the United States from Electromagnetic Pulse (EMP) Attack (EMP Commission), and information in EMP-related military systems and hardening standards, in order to define and release unclassified information on effects and damage characteristics from selected HEMP events, including unclassified composite E1/E2/E3 waveforms. This will answer the question: How much EMP

---

[7] The MEC is an executive-level forum led by the major national security departments and agencies – DHS, DOE, DoD, and the Office of the Director of National Intelligence (ODNI) that coordinates strategic discussion on the utilization of DOE National Laboratory capabilities.

energy is incident on grid systems and how much current and voltage is coupled onto common line and cable configurations?

DTRA has already developed a classified EMP environment standard, MIL-STD-2169C, which can serve as the starting baseline for synthesizing a common set of unclassified standard threat waveforms for use by the electric utility industry. A waveform set for both HEMP fields and coupled currents for common long line installations is indispensable for system assessment and protection engineering.

*Deliverable 1.4.1:* Develop and disseminate unclassified E1 waveforms.
*Due Date:* 12/31/2017

*Deliverable 1.4.2:* Develop and disseminate unclassified composite E1/E2/E3 waveforms.
*Due Date:* 12/31/2019

*Deliverable 1.4.3:* Develop and disseminate a set of unclassified waveforms for coupled currents and voltages for transmission and distribution lines.
*Due Date:* 12/31/2020

## 1.5 Provide an understanding of the susceptibility of specific critical electric grid components to EMP waveforms

System testing is essential for confident prediction of grid failure modes and thresholds as well as for validation of system protection measures. DOE will work with industry, academia, DoD, ODNI, and the DOE National Laboratories to use the results of past tests to supplement the results of present-day electric power grid equipment and sub-systems testing to identify the test waveform voltage and current characteristics, as well as the range in the levels of incident EMP (e.g., kilovolts per meter) and absorbed energy (e.g., joules) and failure modes that disrupt, damage, or destroy critical equipment or sub-systems. Previously determined levels of energy, if any, need to be reviewed, refined, and improved upon with the latest data from tests and models. Because of the cost and limited supply of test data, it is important that DOE facilitate data sharing among government agencies and the utility industry. To the extent possible, DOE will provide test waveforms and system response information in unclassified formats to enable maximum access by the utility industry.

*Deliverable 1.5.1:* Develop a report that highlights past test results, including data sheets showing the estimated levels of EMP that various equipment and sub-systems can withstand, as necessary to supplement current data available from equipment suppliers.
*Due Date:* 05/31/2019 for the report. The data sheets will be released as completed.

## 1.6 Evaluate interactive EMP system and component modeling capabilities

System and component modeling is important for infrastructure impact assessments and design of enhanced protection. Models of the bulk power system and critical components have been developed by government, industry, universities, and commercial firms, but these are limited in scope. Comprehensive models should include the transmission grid, the lower-voltage distribution system as it reacts differently to EMP, power generation plants which are very complex to model and have largely been excluded, and new power system technologies such as solar, wind, modular nuclear reactors, distributed generation networks, and their associated electronics. An evaluation and comparison is needed of selected existing models that are used to estimate impacts to the electric power grid from an EMP event. DOE will then determine the necessary R&D to improve (or replace) these models to more accurately estimate the effects and impacts of EMP on the electric power grid, including generation assets and system load.

Since the simulators used in EMP tests have exposure areas that can accommodate single locations only (i.e., network node systems such as generators, transformers, and control rooms), the ultimate assessment of EMP effects on the grid must rely on modeling the behavior of the larger grid networks based on single node test data. Furthermore, existing grid models are limited in scope in terms of network size incorporated and their ability to simulate the effects of composite E1/E2/E3 waveforms. Many existing models have not been validated experimentally. Test data-based models are needed to gain confidence in prediction of EMP impacts and the effectiveness of grid protection options.

*Deliverable 1.6.1:* Develop a report on the evaluation and comparison of existing EMP models of EMP effects, coupling, and impacts, including recommended areas where new models or validation are needed, or where existing models should be refined.
*Due Date:* 03/31/2018

## 1.7 Develop realistic risk-based EMP planning scenarios for use by industry for planning purposes and assess/model expected damage for each scenario

The universe of possible composite E1/E2/E3 waveforms is large. For the purposes of *Deliverable 1.7.1,* a small set of these will be defined against which DOE can evaluate the susceptibility of critical grid components (*Deliverable 1.7.2*) and have input to models of the interaction between various EMP waveforms and grid systems (*Deliverable 1.7.3*). Additionally, a HEMP scenario is not among the set of 15 planning scenarios issued by the Department of Homeland Security (DHS). To fill the void, DOE in collaboration with the DOE National Laboratories and DHS will establish a range of EMP scenarios (e.g., height of burst, yield, and expected geographic coverage) of concern and map their respective impacts on the electric power grid and interdependent infrastructures.

*Deliverable 1.7.1:* In coordination with DHS, develop a set of EMP planning scenarios that can serve as the basis for threat waveform specifications and assessments of EMP impacts and protection requirements for the grid as well as supporting infrastructures.
*Due Date:* 10/31/2017

*Deliverable 1.7.2:* In coordination with DHS and industry partners, use the EMP planning scenarios of concern as inputs into available models of EMP impacts to the electric grid. The results will be analyzed.
*Due Date:* 10/31/2019

# DOE Electromagnetic Pulse Resilience Action Plan

*Deliverable 1.7.3:* In coordination with DHS, issue a report on the findings from the analysis on the use of the EMP planning scenarios to model EMP impacts to the electric grid.

> *Due Date:* 01/31/2020

## 1.8 Report on potential issues of concern for critical infrastructure from the loss of off-site utility power from EMP

EMP may cause extended loss of off-site utility power to many critical infrastructure facilities in all sectors such as telecommunications assets, hospitals, military bases, nuclear power plants, etc. Federal, State, and local laws, do not generally require owners and operators of these key facilities to address long-term power outages, i.e., most cannot confidently be run for more than a few days on backup power. To ensure the continued functioning of critical facilities will require either protecting off-site power sources or protecting back up power systems and assuring that there is on-site generator fuel supply for extended periods. It will be important to test the survivability of emergency generators to EMP effects.

*Deliverable 1.8.1:* Assess the impacts of EMP on generators commonly used for backup power generation and prepare a report on issues, concerns, and potential mitigation and protection options to ensure critical assets can continue to safely function during a long term power outage due to EMP.

> *Due Date:* 12/31/2018

## 2. Identify Priority Infrastructure

In a world in which the threats to and the vulnerabilities of the electric infrastructure exceed the financial ability to protect against all eventualities, effective protection, mitigation, response, and recovery strategies depend on prioritized resource allocation. To do this, it is important to identify which functions are most critical for both normal electric power grid operation and recovery operations and then determine which components are essential to ensuring those functions will survive. This is a non-trivial task. Damage to one part of the energy infrastructure may have cascading effects in other parts—or not. Uneven levels of resiliency, different equipment, geography, temperature, age, all affect how different parts of the grid respond to different insults.

Most of the work in identifying priority infrastructure has been and will continue to be done by industry through industry analysis and industry forums, and in compliance with the reliability standards of the North American Electric Reliability Corporation (NERC) and the Federal Energy Regulatory Commission (FERC). Additional efforts in this area fall under areas of responsibility of FERC, DHS, and/or the owners and operators themselves.

Owners and operators typically have the best understanding of their systems and are well positioned to identify *their* priority infrastructure. However, these owner/operator priorities may not be aware of nor take into consideration national security concerns, other national and regional interests or the interests of other entities. For this reason, the Federal government has a critical role in identifying priority infrastructure in the electric sector. DOE, as the sector specific agency for the energy sector, has a critical action item to support this strategic goal of identifying priority infrastructure. DOE has an ongoing role to work with all stakeholders to evaluate how all of the objectives under this goal are currently being met and to provide recommendations for improvements.

The following objectives support the joint goal of identifying priority infrastructure for protection, mitigation, response, and recovery:

- Identify critical infrastructure and functions.
- Develop guidance on priority setting.
- Enable sharing of damage assessments to allow refinements in priorities.

### Action Item for Goal 2

### 2.1 Identify and evaluate methodologies for identifying critical infrastructure and functions and any differences related to EMP

Because protection of every component of the electric power grid is impractical, it will be important to develop a risk-based approach to identify the subset of systems and components that are *both* of critical importance to system operation and most susceptible to EMP insult. DOE will work with FERC, DHS, and industry to review and evaluate methodologies used to identify critical, and potentially susceptible, assets, nodes, and systems—and their failure consequences.

*Deliverable 2.1.1:* Prepare a report that identifies and evaluates methodologies for identifying critical infrastructure, reviews findings and includes recommendations.
*Due Date:* 03/31/2017

*Deliverable 2.1.2:* Collaborate with FERC, DHS, and industry to improve methodologies as recommended in the report to reflect changing technologies and conditions.
*Due Date:* 09/30/2020

# 3. Test and Promote Mitigation and Protection Approaches

In addition to understanding how EMP effects may propagate through an electric grid, it is important to understand how individual mitigation strategies and technologies can best contribute to resilience. Research must be conducted to decrease risks inherent in some mitigation and protection approaches. Scientifically validated data must be made available to owners and operators so limited resources can be efficiently applied to risk-based decisions to reduce the consequences of an EMP event through hardening and other methods, rather than focusing on the ability to respond and recover after an incident. Testing by DOE National Laboratories and others will be vital to providing the Nation with information on the effectiveness of different protection techniques.

The most detailed HEMP testing has been performed on military communication and weapon systems, not on high voltage systems essential to electricity generation, transmission, and distribution. Observed HEMP impacts from the high altitude atmospheric nuclear tests conducted by the United States in 1958 and 1962 include system effects observations with little or no available information on HEMP stress levels. Still, to best leverage limited resources, existing test data used in developing military standard EMP protection benchmarks, will be included as a baseline to identify gaps in testing and inform hardening principles and possible protection strategies.

The actions described in this section of the plan support the following objectives for improving EMP protection and mitigation laid out in the Joint Strategy:

- Understand how to best reduce vulnerabilities to EMP.
- Identify new approaches to protection and mitigation.
- Develop, maintain, and protect stockpiles of vulnerable components.
- Develop mitigation plans for operational actions when EMP warnings are available.

## Action Items for Goal 3

### 3.1 Establish a national capability to conduct EMP testing of grid components, systems, and protection technologies

DOE, in consultation with public/private industry partners, will develop a national capability to test and measure impacts to electric power grid components and equipment to composite waveforms that include E1, E2, and E3, as established under Action Item 1.4. Systems must be tested in realistic configurations including various levels of load under energized conditions and mimic industry practices as much as practicable. Test objectives also include a database of measurement data for validating modeling and simulation tools in the future. The test results can validate (or lead to updating of) the report and data sheets created under Action Item 1.5.

*Deliverable 3.1.1:* Develop and validate EMP test requirements, including design and planning considerations.
*Due Date:* 09/30/2018

# DOE Electromagnetic Pulse Resilience Action Plan

*Deliverable 3.1.2:* Advance long-term capabilities for providing testing of individual electric components and the grid system as a whole in a realistic environment.
*Due Date:* 12/31/2018

*Deliverable 3.1.3:* Document test results of individual components and appropriately disseminate analysis describing vulnerabilities and impacts, which may include disruption thresholds and points at which components and equipment are damaged or destroyed.
*Due Date:* 06/30/2019

*Deliverable 3.1.4:* Document test results of the electric grid as a system and validate models for industry use.
*Due Date:* 06/30/2020

## 3.2 Understand the limits and benefits of islanding as an EMP protection strategy.

DOE, in coordination with NERC and its technical committees and subcommittees and the DOE National Laboratories, will assess the risks and benefits of islanding portions of electric power grid as a strategy to prevent or mitigate the impacts of cascading outages. The benefits of grid islanding prior to a HEMP event are uncertain and require further research. Breaking the grid into pre-planned islands on warning has risks but could reduce HEMP cascading impacts and facilitate recovery operations. DOE will research and assess various control options (i.e., manual, automated, etc.) of islanding the grid and produce a report on effectiveness as a prevention and/or mitigation strategy.

*Deliverable 3.2.1:* Develop a study on the options available to island the grid and report on the effectiveness as a prevention and/or mitigation strategy including costs, benefits, and implementation feasibility of islanding in response to an EMP.
*Due Date:* 06/30/2019

## 3.3 Validate mitigation and protection strategies

Although protection engineering practices are well-known and demonstrated for communication and control equipment and facilities, the same is not true for high voltage substation and generation plant equipment. DOD's protection for communication and control systems may not be affordable for some electric power grid facilities and systems, so research on the availability and effectiveness of lower cost techniques and temporary mitigation measures is needed. DOE will work with NERC, FERC, DHS, DoD, and industry to identify and promote effective practices within the electric industry for EMP impact mitigation and protection of individual components, equipment, nodes (e.g., substations), and the system as a whole. The focus will be on the most critical and vulnerable components to EMP, including assets critical for a restart of an electric power grid—as determined from the results of Action Item 3.1.

*Deliverable 3.3.1:* Develop a report identifying and evaluating effective mitigation and protection measures for different components, equipment, and sub-systems.
*Due Date:* 12/31/2020

# DOE Electromagnetic Pulse Resilience Action Plan

## 3.4 Analyze the need for a pilot program to harden substations to a range of EMP scenarios

DOE will analyze the need for a pilot program to harden substations and generation stations to a range of EMP scenarios, and will evaluate the effectiveness of hardening measures. A pilot program will conduct tests on an energized test electric power grid, including high-speed compression networks, for various realistic EMP events. Tests will consider overlap with GMD to avoid duplication of effort by protecting against both threats/hazards when designing and deploying electric systems.

*Deliverable 3.4.1:* Develop a report and project timeline to assess the feasibility of running field tests of different hardening techniques for a set of EMP scenarios.

*Due Date:* 09/30/2021

# 4. Enhance Response and Recovery Capabilities to an EMP Attack

HEMP disruption and damage to the electric grid could be quite extensive, both in terms of area coverage and of duration. Except for certain critical military assets, existing lightning protection, and some pilot hardening against GMD threats, critical national infrastructure remains largely unprotected from EMP threats. As mentioned earlier, however, low altitude or surface bursts are anticipated to have EMP consequences limited to regional or localized impact—analogous to those of a significant storm. This said, the nature of the damage to the grid and supporting technology would be very different in the case of a HEMP: far more damage to electronics would be expected as opposed to gross physical damage (e.g., utility poles broken and power lines down) from an EMP than a storm. EMP damage is often not highly visible, putting a premium on electronic system failure diagnostics. Additionally, in the case of EMP and depending on the magnitude of the pulse, some important equipment that would be permanently destroyed by a storm would only be tripped off but not destroyed, thus easing recovery. Finally, EMPs would likely impact many of the consumer and commercial electronics powered by the grid, and these also would be affected simultaneously in an EMP event.

While many of the activities that can be pursued to improve response capabilities are the same regardless of cause—developing good state and regional plans, conducting and participating in emergency response exercises—a few aspects are different, as noted above. Devising plans to respond and recover the electric grid is best conducted by the owners and operators of the infrastructure; however the government can assist by providing information and focusing discussion on those consequences that differentiate the EMP threat. The actions identified in this plan focus on those efforts that will be pursued specifically in light of EMP effects.

The following objectives support the joint goal of enhancing response and recovery capabilities:

- Provide guidance for the development, exercise, evaluation, and improvement of both response and recovery plans.
- Develop a capability to quickly assess damage from an EMP attack.
- Provide notification of an EMP attack.
- Ensure the survivability of interoperable communications systems during and after an EMP.
- Set realistic power-restoration priorities and expectations.

## Action Items for Goal 4

### 4.1 Familiarize the community to the unique challenges of recovering from EMP-induced damage

DOE will develop materials identifying unique challenges of recovering from EMP that can be used in training modules and/or in preparing EMP exercises. Exercises are extremely important to the HEMP planning process to enable utilities, public officials, first responders, and threat experts to cross-couple and parallel-process the activities essential for pre-event preparation and post-event recovery. Exercises are also an important part of the education process since many utilities public officials and first responders are unaware of HEMP threats and consequences. DOE will lead or support cross-sector EMP exercises with DHS, NERC, FERC, DOD, the Federal Emergency Management Agency (FEMA), State officials, and industry to provide understanding of how EMP damage differs from more traditional damage to the grid, and clarify the roles each plays during and after an EMP event. The existence and adequacy of Continuity of Operations Plans (COOP) should be evaluated.

*Deliverable 4.1.1:* Develop an EMP training and exercise module to identify unique recovery challenges after an EMP based on hypothetical waveform information developed as a result of Goal 1 for use in national exercise scenarios.
*Due Date:* 12/31/2019

*Deliverable 4.1.2:* Adapt one or more DOE-hosted exercises to involve an EMP scenario.
*Due Date:* 06/30/2020

## 4.2 Explore the possibility of providing industry with warning and alert data regarding potential and actual EMP attacks on the United States

Warning of impending EMP attack would offer utilities time to take operational actions that could significantly reduce harmful impacts to their systems. Although HEMP warning times will be minutes at best, there are field-expedient actions (e.g., equipment power cutoff and line re-routes and disconnects) that can help mitigate HEMP effects and expedite recovery. Post-attack awareness would also be of enormous value to utilities as they initiate recovery from EMP-induced power outages. DOE will meet with officials at U.S. Northern Command (USNORTHCOM) to explore a possible approach related to pre- and post-attack warning.

*Deliverable 4.2.1:* Meet with appropriate government departments and agencies (such as USNORTHCOM) to explore the possibility of timely notification(s) of impending EMP events to the emergency operations centers of electric power grid owners/operators and DOE.
*Due Date:* 06/30/2018

## 4.3 Understand the unique profile of EMP-induced damage

EMPs will have a very different damage footprint than more typical natural disasters or cyber events or physical attacks. The expectation would be for more compromise of electronics (from the E1 portion of the waveform), of remote communication and control systems, and to computer systems (from the E1 portion of the waveform). The expectation would be for less gross physical damage, and in some cases, systems that shut down (trip off-line) but experience no permanent damage. Because EMP damage is often not externally visible, electronic system failure diagnostics capabilities will be important. Understanding, at a detailed level, the unique footprint of E1/E2/E3 damage will be critical to the development of good protection and mitigation strategies and will illuminate the potential need stockpiling additional components.

*Deliverable 4.3.1:* Conduct an analysis of the unique footprint of E1/E2/E3 damage at a level of detail that informs protection and mitigation strategies and the need to stockpile additional components to facilitate recovery.
*Due Date:* 12/31/2020

## 4.4 Understand the unique challenges of black starts after EMP-induced damage

While many large utilities have black-start plans and capabilities based on more typical triggering events, the black start capabilities are usually not themselves protected from EMPs. It is also the case that in the event of a grid failure collapse due to EMP, it is likely that the telecommunications needed to restore the grid may also be inoperable. Finally, much of the electrical equipment powered by the affected portion of the grid may similarly be damaged and will affect the availability of the load necessary to balance the system when restarting generation stations. The interaction of these circumstances will create a unique set of challenges that are now only poorly understood.

*Deliverable 4.4.1:* Analyze the unique challenges facing utilities attempting a black start following an EMP-induced damage.
*Due Date:* 06/30/2020

*Deliverable 4.4.2:* Work with industry and related organizations to encourage owners and operators to develop EMP annexes to their response and recovery plans that incorporate effective practices to mitigate damage and expedite restoration and recovery from an EMP event.
*Due Date:* 06/30/2021

# 5. Share Best Practices Across Government and Industry, Nationally and Internationally

Threats posed by EMP are not limited to the electricity subsector, nor to the United States. Several nations have also been researching HEMP and GMD effects, notably the United Kingdom, Switzerland, Sweden, and Israel. The United States can benefit from their experience. International sharing of protection methods and lessons learned will help ensure that effective, demonstrated HEMP protection practices are implemented. International cooperation is especially important to ensure coordinated protection of the North American electric grid which spans Canada, the United States, and parts of Mexico.

Similarly, there is benefit from the broad sharing of a common, vetted technical understanding of the E1/E2/E3 waveforms created by the most likely threats and their potential impact on electronics. This information will not only benefit the electricity subsector, but will also be relevant to all sectors that are dependent on electronics susceptible to EMP damage. This includes, but is not limited to the financial, telecommunications, and transportation sectors.

The following objectives from the Joint Strategy support the goal of increasing broad-based information sharing:

- Build international support and policies for information sharing.
- Share the results of analyses and testing.
- Investigate and share the findings of any EMP incidents.
- Promote a collaborative international approach to preparedness for EMP events.

## Action Items for Goal 5

### 5.1 Share EMP information and best practices with other sectors

DOE will work closely through the Energy Government Coordinating Council (EGCC) to identify other interagency partners to share the best practices of the efforts described earlier in this Action Plan.

*Deliverable 5.1.1:* Share information with the EGCC and other sectors at EGCC meetings and other fora.
*Due Date:* 09/30/2018

### 5.2 Share EMP information and best practices with other nations

DOE will work closely with international partners (government and utility officials) to share effective practices on EMP electric power grid resilience and coordinate on the large range of EMP issues.

*Deliverable 5.2.1:* Meet with foreign government officials and other organizations to share information on EMP resilience practices in unclassified and classified environments and to bring information back to other U.S. partners.
*Due Date:* 09/30/2018

## Appendix A: Chronological List of Deliverables

| Deliverable | Due Date |
| --- | --- |
| *1.2.1:* Establish a working group of the Mission Execution Council to identify current gaps in EMP knowledge among the National Laboratories and other Federal agencies. | 10/31/2016 |
| *1.1.1:* Maintain classified and unclassified briefing materials that address the current understanding of the potential impacts of high and low impact EMPs on the electric grid. | 12/31/2016 |
| *1.2.2:* Produce a report documenting MEC findings. | 12/31/2016 |
| *1.3.1:* Establish an EMP information working group in coordination with EPRI, the ESCC, and appropriate stakeholders. | 12/31/2016 |
| *1.1.2:* Create a schedule of industry, interagency, and cross-sector briefings using these materials. | 03/31/2017 |
| *2.1.1:* Prepare a report that identifies and evaluates methodologies for identifying critical infrastructure, reviews findings and includes recommendations. | 03/31/2017 |
| *1.7.1:* In coordination with DHS, develop a set of EMP planning scenarios that can serve as the basis for threat waveform specifications and assessments of EMP impacts and protection requirements for the grid as well as supporting infrastructures. | 10/31/2017 |
| *1.4.1:* Develop and disseminate unclassified E1 waveforms. | 12/31/2017 |
| *1.6.1:* Develop a report on the evaluation and comparison of existing EMP models of EMP effects, coupling, and impacts, including recommended areas where new models or validation are needed, or where existing models should be refined. | 03/31/2018 |
| *4.2.1:* Meet with appropriate government departments and agencies (such as USNORTHCOM) to explore the possibility of timely notification(s) of impending EMP events to the emergency operations centers of electric power grid owners/operators and DOE. | 06/30/2018 |
| *3.1.1:* Develop and validate EMP test requirements, including design and planning considerations. | 09/30/2018 |
| *5.1.1:* Share information with the EGCC and other sectors at EGCC meetings and other fora. | 09/30/2018 |
| *5.2.1:* Meet with foreign government officials and other organizations to share information on EMP resilience practices in unclassified and classified environments and to bring information back to other U.S. partners. | 09/30/2018 |
| *1.8.1:* Assess the impacts of EMP on generators commonly used for backup power generation and prepare a report on issues, concerns, and potential mitigation and protection options to ensure critical assets can continue to safely function during a long term power outage due to EMP. | 12/31/2018 |
| *3.1.2:* Advance long-term capabilities for providing testing of individual electric components and the grid system as a whole in a realistic environment. | 12/31/2018 |
| *1.5.1:* Develop a report that highlights past test results, including data sheets showing the estimated levels of EMP that various equipment and sub-systems can withstand, as necessary to supplement current data available from equipment suppliers. | 05/31/2019 |
| *3.1.3:* Document test results of individual components and appropriately disseminate analysis describing vulnerabilities and impacts, which may include disruption thresholds and points at which components and equipment are damaged or destroyed. | 06/30/2019 |
| *3.2.1:* Develop a study on the options available to island the grid and report on the effectiveness as a prevention and/or mitigation strategy including costs, benefits, and implementation feasibility of islanding in response to an EMP. | 06/30/2019 |

# DOE Electromagnetic Pulse Resilience Action Plan

| Deliverable | Due Date |
| --- | --- |
| *1.7.2:* In coordination with DHS and industry partners, use the EMP planning scenarios of concern as inputs into available models of EMP impacts to the electric grid. The results will be analyzed. | 10/31/2019 |
| *1.4.2:* Develop and disseminate unclassified composite E1/E2/E3 waveforms. | 12/31/2019 |
| *4.1.1:* Develop an EMP training and exercise module to identify unique recovery challenges after an EMP based on hypothetical waveform information developed as a result of Goal 1 for use in national exercise scenarios. | 12/31/2019 |
| *1.7.3:* In coordination with DHS, issue a report on the findings from the analysis on the use of the EMP planning scenarios to model EMP impacts to the electric grid. | 01/31/2020 |
| *3.1.4:* Document test results of the electric grid as a system and validate models for industry use. | 06/30/2020 |
| *4.1.2:* Adapt one or more DOE-hosted exercises to involve an EMP scenario. | 06/30/2020 |
| *4.4.1:* Analyze the unique challenges facing utilities attempting a black start following an EMP-induced damage. | 06/30/2020 |
| *2.1.2:* Collaborate with FERC, DHS, and industry to improve methodologies as recommended in the report to reflect changing technologies and conditions. | 09/30/2020 |
| *1.4.3:* Develop and disseminate a set of unclassified waveforms for coupled currents and voltages for transmission and distribution lines. | 12/31/2020 |
| *3.3.1:* Develop a report identifying and evaluating effective mitigation and protection measures for different components, equipment, and sub-systems. | 12/31/2020 |
| *4.3.1:* Conduct an analysis of the unique footprint of E1/E2/E3 damage at a level of detail that informs protection and mitigation strategies and the need to stockpile additional components to facilitate recovery. | 12/31/2020 |
| *4.4.2:* Work with industry and related organizations to encourage owners and operators to develop EMP annexes to their response and recovery plans that incorporate effective practices to mitigate damage and expedite restoration and recovery from an EMP event. | 06/30/2021 |
| *3.4.1:* Develop a report and project timeline to assess the feasibility of running field tests of different hardening techniques for a set of EMP scenarios. | 09/30/2021 |

www.ingramcontent.com/pod-product-compliance
Lightning Source LLC
Chambersburg PA
CBHW040254240726
48664CB00001B/395